OPEN AIR BINDERY

Open Air Bindery

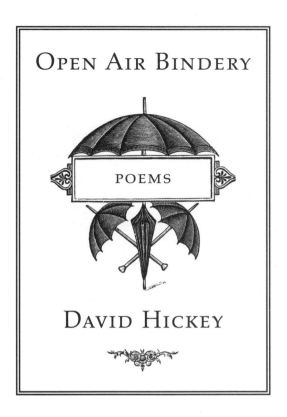

POEMS

David Hickey

BIBLIOASIS

FIRST EDITION

Library and Archives Canada Cataloguing in Publication

Hickey, David, 1977-
        Open air bindery / David Hickey.

Poems.
ISBN 978-1-926845-24-1

        I. Title.

PS8615.I34O64 2011   C811'.6   C2011-900986-2

Canada Council   Conseil des Arts
for the Arts   du Canada

Canadian   Patrimoine
Heritage   canadien

ONTARIO ARTS COUNCIL
CONSEIL DES ARTS DE L'ONTARIO

Biblioasis acknowledges the ongoing financial support of the
Government of Canada through The Canada Council for the Arts,
Canadian Heritage, the Book Publishing Industry Development
Program (BPIDP); and the Government of Ontario through the
Ontario Arts Council.

PRINTED AND BOUND IN CANADA

for Chris and Sue—
two shoo-ins for the sibling hall of fame

Contents

Open Voyage / 11

Hinterland Who's Who

X-Ray / 15

The Garden Shed / 16

Hinterland Who's Who / 18

Aubade / 20

Suburbia the Beautiful / 21

The White Papers / 24

Public Transit / 26

Footnote to the Book of Moonlight / 27

Restrictive Covenants

Short Lives / 31

The Astronomer's Apology / 33

A Brief History of Human Longing / 34

The Lobster Pound Keeper Ponders the Afterlife / 35

Message in a Bottle / 36

Night Crossing to Prince Edward Island / 37

Bedtime Stories

Oh God, Oh Charlottetown / 43

The Tree of Old Worry / 44

At This Hour / 45

Insomnia Drawings / 46

Once Upon a Business Trip, In Faraway
West Virginia / 48

The Story of Two Horses / 50

At the Waverley Inn / 51

Vespers / 53

Biographies / 54

Snowflake Photography

    Plate 1. / 60

    Plate 2. / 61

    Plate 3. / 62

    Plate 4. / 64

    Plate 5. / 66

    Plate 6. / 68

*Les paysages de nuit ont
envahi les jours.*

—*Louise Bourgeois,* The Insomnia Drawings

Open Voyage

For as long as this painting has hung here,
    the figure living within its framed wooden borders has pushed
      herself

down the Nile, her vessel
    gliding above the bookshelf, past the vase of scissors and pens,

towards the wall's great expanse, that still
    gyprock sea

leading to nowhere
    but the corner of the room where the latex continues
      throughout the house,

intersecting at comfortable angles.
    Just once,

I would like her small boat to crest the wooden waterfall
    of the painting's frame

and circle around me, a red shadow
    staining the eggshell white, a ripple of blue appearing beneath
      her cedar hull

as she parts new waters;
    for her to push around the doorway's frame, to dodge the light
      switch

while a wallflower moon, hiding
    too long now in the cellar, rises over a horizon of dusty

radiators. Or one morning,
    settling myself in for another day's shift, to look up from the
      desk

and find she's gone: receding in the distance,
  a nautical brush mark

miles away, her small ship gliding into the painting's
  canvas, into its beginnings

where she stands, faintly
  stenciled, waiting for the river to be

drawn in her hand, the water's generous gift that will
  lift her into perspective,

the final blackened brush stroke that will
  ferry her into the night.

Hinterland Who's Who

X-Ray

So this is where I've hidden
my ghost, shadow of all

my firsts, essential self
shuttered down to its most

basic pajamas:
I've been looking for you,

ornithological bouquet
blooming in the dark

room of my days,
I've been walking around

in negative,
I've been wondering

how I fit, moony
white, in the wetsuit of my body—

so it's good
to greet you at last,

and to see
there's nothing wrong

with me, nothing
broken, nothing missing

but the wings
of a book

in my hand, nothing
but a little

lamplight
left on inside me.

The Garden Shed

Could I live in this
thing? Good shack, sturdy

shed, reliable
Home Hardware

special, I'll make
a place where the mower

might have been,
one square window

to steam with a kettle
atop a potbelly

stove, beans
and stew when I see

someone coming,
plaid and bad patch

of beard when I don't:
I'm there already,

stupidly proud of my
misery, pulling

cans from an overstocked
pantry, the black flies

threatening me
while I rant against

the covenants
of my old suburban

zone—not
here, not as I set up

on a bluff
near a beach,

eccentric cough
of the cliff, believing

there's a bead
of wind to climb back

with, one knotted
rope that knows

its way down to the water,
and a claystone

rosary still
waiting below.

Hinterland Who's Who

Distant cousin to the broom
closet coaster, the mailbox
mifter, and the winnebago wisp,

the chimney swift is a small, sooty bird
that clings to the bricks of chimneys,
which is why

they call it the chimney
swift, not the telephone wire
warbler or the tall

tree startler; and hardly
ever do they call it
the-little-swat-that-flies-off-with-my-sleep,

the-small-slip-of-somnolence-
lining-my-chimney, the-ball-of-feathers-
for-whom-I'll-cap-the-chimney-

altogether, thereby
evicting the swift without sixty days
notice. Little crematory bird

that breeds in North
America and winters in Peru,
little late shift of wind

whose habitat is already smoke,
I don't care where you go
with my sleep,

just stay there
a good while longer;
and be a smart witness

to what's left of the chimney's
warmth; stay hidden,
and stay ashen,

and I'll meet you there,
however it may
happen, someday on the soft side of masonry.

Aubade

This morning I saw the front
lawn for the first time, I
saw the grass and the garden,

I saw the street and the houses
slowly gain momentum
as they ran down it,

all the magnificent cars
of the century were headed
somewhere, they were

celebrating and they
didn't even know it: they rolled
past, invisible flags waving

from antennas while the wind
confettied the street, and
the front lawn sunned

its brush cut, and the paper
arrived in its plastic.
And even the sky's headlines

seemed happy to see me,
breathless with news
of their little blue world.

Suburbia the Beautiful

There's nothing I
don't know about marigolds.

That's why
I can tell you

the tallest is nodding to the second-
in-command

in a small
battalion of summer.

That's why
they're paused and sympathetic

next to the patio lattice.
That's why

you should really
fix your patio lattice.

The stop sign
reddens the street.

The raccoon
machetes the hedge.

And the paperboy
you forgot to pay

last week skirts
the sidewalk's edge,

fielding a fly ball
deeper and

deeper in the canola fields
of his mind. Only

he's never seen canola,
so that's why

the fly ball never lands.
(There's nothing

I don't know
about fly balls that never

land.) That's why
the sun sets

the way that it does
well past the gates of evening.

That's why
the garage doors

close the way that they do,
that's why

they wave slowly
goodnight,

that's why
the foliage, why

the drawbridge,
and why

the quiet castle.
The pavement rivers

past empty
lots. The lawn

waters itself off to sleep.
And the soft

raft of the day,
it gets lost

in the sea
of the paperboy's

fading
blue denim.

The White Papers

There's this one stack of paper
    going slowly around

your glass desk, and you
    nudge it lovingly

like an overweight kid on skates,
    the kind whose snowsuit

bunches like a pillowcase,
    who lags behind the others,

who grips chairs as though holding
    tight to a forest's wooden

shoulders; whose
    nose runs, whose toque blankets

his forehead and drips
    onto his face, and who looks up

at you, after twenty minutes
    of innocent effort,

having moved just as many
    feet, and with a hard-

won flush to his face,
    has no idea why you station

yourself here, in this
    den of private sector profit,

where, in these days of make-
    believe warnings,

you're really a bit of a pink-
    shirted war profiteer.

Still, you follow the scratchy
    trails that wind

across your desk. And
    sometimes, make

a little space for winter's
    lake to appear.

Public Transit

Standing under my umbrella
the other day, feeling
a little bit like a sporting event

with my own retractable
dome, I wondered what I must
look like from above—

and from below, where the street
seemed to look up from all
places at once: curious,

I suppose, to see what it was
shouldering. And I felt
the wet animals of the hour go

motoring; I felt them
stretch out from the driveways
of the day—small caravans

of soil, set forth,
hours ago, as though
the whole world were waiting.

Footnote to the Book of Moonlight

First published as *The Cotton
Sonnet*, then posthumously

as *The Mineral Thief*,
the book of moonlight never

did appear in paperback.
It was bound in an open air

bindery, just before
the collected sidewalk, just

after the selected raccoon.
In one monograph,

the moon actually dances off
from its own dinner party,

the dishes not done and the guests
still talking, the streetlights

huddled outside, tall
tradesmen gossiping cautiously

about the constellations,
how great the space

between them, how strange
their crooked carpentry.

Of course, that's just one
edition. Others contend

it just sinks back to the suburbs,
the dewy shingles above

the two-car garage
where the moon now

lives, and where it drifts off,
if I remember correctly,

in the night's quiet
library. The wind stopping by

to thumb through it,
then putting it back

when it's done.
See also the moon,

sitting on a shelf,
just out of reach.

Its call number
the square root of one.

Restrictive Covenants

Short Lives

It's a short life to spend
in a urinal. Ten men,

all leaning in,
solemn as a summer funeral,

posed in the basement
of Union Station

and staring forward
in unison, the first position

in a poorly-cast
ballet that ends

without grace or allusion.
And then, drying by

the dyson airblade,
they listen to the wind

in the land where
dryness is king, one

quick slip in
the breeze's back pocket

before shuffling off,
exit stage-left

to whatever
their days will bring.

I tell you all
this, though I don't really

know what it means.
Most days

I'm lost in the staging
of the twentieth-first century.

And never sure
if it's my turn to sing.

The Astronomer's Apology

Sorry for the sound of my steps
on the floor—wherever I
walked, it creaked. There was a new

moon above and I swallowed the dark
(it still comes out now as I speak).
Sorry, too, for the door I didn't quite close;

the cold pulled you out of your sleep.
It's what the new moon does: it
deals out the stars; it dances, it drinks

and it cheats. All day long,
the planet revolved; it turned in
the troposphere's keep. With new moon

above, I swept through the dark. Then
I swept the dark off my feet. Still
I'm sorry, this morning, when

I came back to bed, if my hands had lost
all their heat. It's an old tune, love,

what you lose in the dark,
what follows you back to the sheets.

A Brief History of Human Longing

Chapter One

I borrowed it from the library. It held onto my hand.

Chapter Two

I carried it like a rosary. It was the weight of a wedding band.

Chapter Three

I wore it off to work each day and back again at six.

Chapter Four

It sang out to the mower (the sink I couldn't fix).

Chapter Five

I fell asleep against its font and my sleep was an old green hill.

Chapter Six

I look up sometimes, and see it there.

Epilogue

And farther, farther still.

The Lobster Pound Keeper Ponders the Afterlife

I prefer a harbour in place of a gate, to be sure,
haul me in with another day's catch here

at St. Peter's low wake. They reek of bled fish,
and the shacks, they've lost their stakes,

but old wharves, they're just as you
find them. And however I come ashore is fine

enough here: the ocean was furrowed by
the trawler's great take, and wherever

its passages tried to escape they were lifted
right up, resurrected, you might say,

yanked along like a bad lover's necklace.
So, yes. There isn't anyone, anything

left to tie me. But then I try not to nod off
too worrisome: there's still a few

skippers with teeth, one or two keep a hid
dory down East—say that Kharon,

boy, he's a good cod fisherman.
So never mind the gates and the miracle

of loaves, I'll leave those to the farmers
and businessmen. All I ever wanted

was to break a few waves with
The Susie Kate, a kettle on the stove

and fish from the Strait, and
sure, to stow enough supper for everyone.

Message in a Bottle

At last, you've found me. Or at least the part
I placed here, in hopes of covering some
distance. Let's see: in the horizon's bedtime story,

the waves were in love with the wine cork,
but the bottle made off with the moon. I'm not
making things better by writing this letter.

I can't paddle to sea with a spoon. Let's just say
I was walking the beach, and felt the sweep
of the tide's cold fume. My thoughts were fragile,

so I fit them to glass. It was fast, the wind,
but steady the planks of the shore,
the sea riding bright against the sand's rough bow.

I'm telling you it was hard to let
go of. I'm glad if you're holding it now.

Night Crossing to Prince Edward Island

The car settling onto the bridge,
the water hidden behind

guard rails as if only
the blindfolded could cross,

the pavement running
high over broken

ice: I haven't been here until
now, the passage

foreign each time,
exiting Veterans Highway,

half-expecting
an hour's rest while the boat

empties, and the beams
of travelers grip

the tail lights ahead,
a company moving

predictably as
blue edges a map of land.

⁓

Blue edges a map of land:
it's been how long now

since I held the ferry's
back rail with my hand,

the black and white
of the water and the propeller's

fast bath below?
One foot on the rail, the other

up a few inches or so,
believing I was leaning out

for the song of it,
the steep lure of the ocean cold—

I may have
been ten or eleven

then. I suppose
it doesn't hurt to think so.

~

The car's weight
leaving the bridge, and the low

lights of the village ahead.
I never remember

which way this last ridge
goes. I saw it curl past

a boat coming off
the water once, but that was

another winter, and now
there's just the indifference

of December, doing
its tidal work to the coast.

Still, it's this ambivalent
moon I most know:

it's packed and
cold, and feels as though

it's moving among
the cliff's dark margins,

white given in a second-
guessing of snow,

I'm alone and
looking into my thirty-

third year, and leaning in
to see what I can:

the banks are hidden,
and it's a long way

across, and the fields,
first and last

ferrymen, just lend
their blank stares to my hand.

The beams of travelers
grip the tail lights

ahead. Blue
edges a map of land.

Bedtime Stories

Oh God, Oh Charlottetown

The harbour told me this once.

It told me about a city where the snow drifts
took on the colour of every house

they brushed against,
and the front lawns and the streets were tinted

by the dozens of shades
that clung to the neighborhood

homes. Miraculous,
it said. Snow fell on the rooftops in a way

that made me think
it had always been winter in that city.

Strange, I know, but that's how
it felt. It felt like

the middle of the night, and that, at such an hour,
the lawns and the streets

and the houses were all one,
as if the snow was the work of some

sleepless walker, one
who wore her thoughts through the city

like a scarf around her shoulders,
who gathered them

closer, all the conversations that passed by
single pane windows

disappearing into old drafts, the steady
drift of her footsteps

walking away with their light.

The Tree of Old Worry

If you hang a tire from the tree of old
worry, be careful
how long you swing.

If you build a house in its branches,
its mortgage will
foreclose in a month.

Fat luck, said the broker.
Holding onto a tree for a month.

As for the owl
you spot in its branches,
it's safe to stop saying

hello. As for your canteen
and the tree of old
worry, I'd caution the tea from its leaves.

And as for the canoe
you'd carve from its bark,
I'm told it floats poorly downriver.

Fat luck, said the arborist.
No one remembers
who paddled here last.

No one knows
the next party upriver.

At This Hour

The toilet is also the shell of an animal
whose body fills the house with its
lull, the soft whirl of the bowl

at the streetlights, the silo of an armless
bell. Its handle needs to be pressed
at, needs to be jiggled, needs to be held,

the flush slightly off since water
first fell through its valves just after
the house was built. It arrived

then like a beacon, pink in a pick-up
truck's sky: it appeared complete
with ports for pipes, with factory dust,

the porcelain not yet chipped
from a plumber's impatience. It waits
for new company, new words,

for the shuffle of bare feet in the hall,
a stark figure to stand in the doorway,
swaying a little dance to the darkness.

Insomnia Drawings

Composite sketch by the architect of absent sleep:

here's me by the sink, socklessly dusting

the floor. I select myself a utensil.

I sing myself off to the kettle. I shuffle myself to the
    stove.

Meanwhile the kitchen is

quietly studying its magic, its abracadabra of pots and
    pans,

the collection of soup in the closet.

The faucet plays its favorite trickle,

the late house

casts its clothesline with hopes the wind will run by.

Listen.

    Never mind.

    Little life rafts that sail in the shoals

    of these hours; that's what the kitchen tiles

    will be.

So until the shadowy coast of the morning
  approaches,

a moment or two from the night

sayings of trees:

Rock-a-bye, cradle,

       the kitchen is lean.

When the spoon's an old

       fable, the clock's a lost king.

Once Upon a Business Trip,
In Faraway West Virginia

i.

There was a man who couldn't sleep.
   So he watched a documentary
on water. So he looked out at the freeway,
   and imagined he was a car.

ii.

And he studied the light. He was in luck,
   for he was awash in its glow.
He tanned on the balcony's
   midnight. He addressed the world in his

underwear. He stood there, hanging
   his thoughts out to dry in the wattage of the all-
night sun.

iii.

        There was a hotel
across the street, there was the street,
   there was a sea of light
and a night stop swimming in it.

So that's where he'd eaten,

iv.

the waitress who served him then
   now resting somewhere
      in the great state of West Virginia.

v.

He sat by the television's stream.
It made him think of the hotel
   lobby, of the swans swimming
there, each in a cubical

   pool, floating around in the pale
white boats of their bodies.

He imagined them turning in circles
awhile, their orange rudder feet

   twitching this way
and that, paddles in the pool's marble harmony.

He, too, wanted to paddle
around in his sleep,

   to know the pale white coast of such
company. He wanted

   to swim across the street,
and for another room

vi.

to be waiting on the other side.

He turned off the tv, and standing
there in its momentary

   mirror, what he saw was formless
and empty. He hung his only face

over the surface of its depth. He hovered
   over those waters.

The Story of Two Horses

The first horse had no interest in escaping.
    The second was wearing

its evening clothes. The first looked as though
    it had stolen

through a midnight bakery, so the second was
    brushed with a dusting of flour.

It's like this: the first story is good
    flesh. The second is all fetlock and narrative.

Giddy up, said the car
    as it motioned past the field.

We were late with the day's last requests.

At the Waverley Inn

Spring in Halifax and the bar
goers have broken hibernation,

they're coatless in small canvas
shoes that test the snowless

ground as the sun goes looking
for the other side of the planet,

and the corner tavern signs
its name in neon above the street.

Perched in my citadel,
the world seems well from here.

Whoever says you can't sit
in a nest of pajamas

with an oversized Oscar
Wilde portrait keeping you

company, his hair parted
cleanly more than a century

ago, his face casually certain,
his shirt slow river blue,

they didn't stay here.
But never mind the centuries:

I was standing in the shower
a few minutes ago, wondering

if there could possibly be
nothing lonely about solitude,

if you could just sit in a room
and be content not to dwell

on the absence of others,
and if, once you sit on the edge

of the bed, part of you stays
there, brief impression

in the spread that remains,
you know, long after

it's time to go. If Oscar
Wilde did stay in this room,

the caption should read:
the rest of us stayed here,

too, one solitary tribe under
Wilde's good sleep.

So here's to our drinking
glass, and here's

to our sink. And here's
to our portrait.

And here's to its keep.

Vespers

Whatever arrives at dusk
  doesn't arrive alone:

there's a whole day huddled
  at its wings, and the hours follow

thereafter, faraway
  from the kingdom of second thought

where now
  there's just the first thought

repeating: evening, light
  traveler coming from market,

expected guest
  whose meal is always warming,

I'm remembering
  a story

that was told late at our door—
  it was

clothed in old
  tales from your village.

Biographies

You're waiting for a train heading east:
it's one you've taken before, so

often the novelty long since leapt
to the tracks, spun under by the weight

of its passengers. You're enjoying this
image of yourself, of one who no longer

believes the biography of the train is
a brief history of human longing,

faithless that desire is continuous,
sinuously moving from station to station.

And boarding the train you know
you'll join the slow parade of those

dressed with devices that disperse them
elsewhere, you've sat uncomfortably

beside their conversations—those
who travel so often, disclose

too much as they go. But for now,
you're still in Union Station, and rising

through an angled gap to the rails,
you're sharing an escalator stair

with a woman who just let go of the man
still waiting below, and you only

noticed their affection
because they seemed so out-of-place

underground, in the impatience
of the mid-winter cold. A brief history

of human longing: she waves
to the security camera, one last goodbye

from the platform hold, and he stands
at the foot of a vanishing stair.

Now you see them, now you don't.

Snowflake Photography

An eager voice emerges from within you (I hear it now, these fifty odd years since it first shook the snow-covered tree branches of myself), "How is all this to be done?" You know by now that this is no simple matter. But I would hope you take the pages to come as you would the hand of a guide, one who knows the path through the woods, even as he travels it in the dark. And know too that there will be time to reflect; for, like the astronomer who waits in patience for the clouds to clear, the snow crystal photographer also stands with his mind open to the sky, though certainly in hopes of different results. No matter. Dress to your warmest. Gather up your things. And surely, when the moment presents itself, you will most certainly be prepared.

—The Snowflake Photographer's Field Guide

Plate 1.

Begin with a brief interlude
in which the woman you wake up to

offers an unusual gift:
lifting the book before you,

she waves a few snowflakes in the air.
Small instances of colliding

light, each pronunciation dances
as she points to its name

on the page. Wilson Alwyn Bentley
spent a lifetime cataloguing

crystals, and now she's packing
your bags for the icicle

museum, the two of you tourists
in a miniature ice age:

"Imagine," she says,
holding each one up to the light,

"What the world
looks like inside one."

Plate 2.

What the world looks like
inside of one: it's your third winter

together, and even though
you've dug your tools

from the shed, your proposal is
still an unfinished

device, a series of well-
meaning parts

in quiet need of assembling.
You look at her,

marvel at how she studies
each short lifetime

framed in a frozen
ecology. It should be

as easy as this, a question
coming easily

as clouds, you
with the right tool and

the sky's small
bolts in your hand.

Plate 3.

Hypothesis. What the world
  could look like

inside of one: the sky tumbles
  inside its own

quiet: in a restless mid-winter's
  sleep, in drifts, in

one or two moments
  past midnight when you feel

yourself piloting to Earth,
  you and the universe's tidy

store of time tucked inside
  a snowflake, newly

blessed with seats
  and invisible parachutes.

The frost buckles you in
  as Bentley appears

at your side, unruffled
  by his new-found company,

and so the two of you
  float over evening forests

(he in his derby hat,
  you in your toque), opening

now and then the manual
  you find in the basket:

The Unwritten
   Book of Snowflakes,

it's without
   pictures or words; just pages

and pages of white,
   which is what the world

looks like where
   you're sitting: pages

and pages of white,
   the work of some careful

pressman minding
   his craft

as he lays
   out the fields below.

Plate 4.

Bentley stands before you,
   unmarried in the night-time

forest. He's pondering
   the tripod's trick geometry,

the difficulty of catching
   each flake in the smoky

flash. Bentley and his
   trouble framing each crystal,

his frostbit hands
   resting on the camera's cold

metal. Bentley
   and bachelorhood.

Bentley as he tells you
   about the faithful of one

mountainside church,
   how its followers sit outside

each snowfall,
   believing

the words of their Saviour
   dwell in each falling

crystal. As he takes
   your picture you wonder

if he invented them
   just now, fabricated

these followers,
  lit candles for them

in a church of ice,
  but later you find yourself

imagining their winter
  gardens, carrots and peas

in a draughty pantry.
  You peek into their stone

houses, find men
  warming the arthritic

hands of their wives,
  children gripped by

the icicle thoughts
  of their sleep. And all

around them smokeless
  chimneys come up

for air in the sky,
  each soot mouth

open to the moon's
  dark infancy, the moon

tucked in its black
  flannel bed

sheet, the moon rolling over
  once in the night.

Plate 5.

Falling asleep by a living room fire,
   Bentley's arms hold open

an album of snowflakes.
   Your thoughts have brought him

here, having trudged across
   the night's wide

aperture. He's telling you
   it's not true so many words for snow

fall from arctic
   clouds: it's just a traveler's

misunderstanding, and having spent
   too long in such wistful

woods, he's tired of those
   empty countries.

His body, slumped in his chair,
   looks as fragile

as the snow in his pictures.
   He could be thinking of summer,

how so little
   falls through that season,

or autumn, perhaps,
   with those countless

leaves, the forest's
   reliable precipitation.

As he nods off, you picture
   him as a single

white flake, alone in the sky's
   empty darkroom.

You picture him
   held above the stop bath's

lake, in the dictates
   of downward migration.

Plate 6.

What the world looks like
    inside of one:

late afternoon, and Bentley's
    books are keeping

you company: they rest on a century-
    old table, offering

their testimony to the pine's
    rivered grain.

You're waiting
    among these old

wooden channels,
    here in the household inlet

where the table charts
    its own passage,

deep within the vessel of its age.
    You're reading how

you can't know
    enough to get married,

any more than you might
    predict a surprise.

But there she is now,
    coming up the walk, surrounded by

the predictable
    surprise that it's snowing

(just one word
    outside). And you can see

how, from above
    the streetlight's waver,

it's coming towards
    the house in every possible

way: the snow, taking its
    time, covering

the roadside trees
    in forms of its careful willing:

the snow, gesturing
    down to earth,

unveiling new
    shapes for all that it finds

here in the oldest
    of botanies.

Acknowledgements

Versions of these poems appeared in *CV2*, *Rampike*, and *CNQ*.

"Snowflake Photography" was first published as a chipbook (not to be confused with its big cousin, the chapbook) by Little Fishcart Press.

A broadside of "Suburbia the Beautiful" was printed as a local fundraiser for the League of Canadian Poets.

My thanks to everyone who saw these poems into print, especially Judy Gaudet and Jeramy Dodds.

John MacKenzie, Bryce Traister, John Smith, Charmaine Cadeau, Richard Lemm, Katia Grubisic, Rebecca Campbell, and Ross Leckie—your collective intellect could power cities. My gratitude for the many conversations that helped shape this book.

For reading these poems with a sharp pencil, thanks to Tina Northrup, Tara Murphy, Nina Budabin McQuown, and Eric Ormsby.

The book of moonlight is courtesy of Wallace Stevens, by way of Don McKay.

"Oh God Oh Charlottetown" is from Al Purdy's *Naked with Summer in Your Mouth*.

A line from Wendell Berry's essay, "People, Land, and Community," appears in the last section of "Snowflake Photography."

The "wattage of the all-night sun" is on loan from Leslie C. Peltier's *Starlight Nights*.

To the Ontario Arts Council, and to the Canada Council for the Arts, my deep gratitude for support at various times.

To Dan Wells, for making this (and other miracles) happen.

Erica Leighton, for outwitting me at every turn.

And my family, for having such great snowball fights.

David Hickey grew up on Prince Edward Island, in western Labrador, and along the north shore of Quebec. A past recipient of the Milton Acorn Prize and the Ralph Gustafson Prize, his first book of poetry, *In the Lights of a Midnight Plow*, was a finalist for the Gerald Lampert Award. An avid backyard astronomer, he now lives in London, Ontario.